GRILLING 101

USING THE GRILL IS EASY. DISCOVER DELICIOUS GRILLED MEATS AND VEGETABLES WITH EASY GRILLING RECIPES

By
BookSumo Press
Copyright © by Saxonberg Associates

Published by
BookSumo Press, a DBA of Saxonberg Associates
http://www.booksumo.com/

ABOUT THE AUTHOR.

BookSumo Press is a publisher of unique, easy, and healthy cookbooks.

Our cookbooks span all topics and all subjects. If you want a deep dive into the possibilities of cooking with any type of ingredient. Then BookSumo Press is your go to place for robust yet simple and delicious cookbooks and recipes. Whether you are looking for great tasting pressure cooker recipes or authentic ethic and cultural food. BookSumo Press has a delicious and easy cookbook for you.

With simple ingredients, and even simpler step-by-step instructions BookSumo cookbooks get everyone in the kitchen chefing delicious meals.

BookSumo is an independent publisher of books operating in the beautiful Garden State (NJ) and our team of chefs and kitchen experts are here to teach, eat, and be merry!

INTRODUCTION

Welcome to *The Effortless Chef Series*! Thank you for taking the time to purchase this cookbook.

Come take a journey into the delights of easy cooking. The point of this cookbook and all BookSumo Press cookbooks is to exemplify the effortless nature of cooking simply.

In this book we focus on Grilling. You will find that even though the recipes are simple, the taste of the dishes are quite amazing.

So will you take an adventure in simple cooking? If the answer is yes please consult the table of contents to find the dishes you are most interested in.

Once you are ready, jump right in and start cooking.

— BookSumo Press

TABLE OF CONTENTS

ANY ISSUES? CONTACT US

If you find that something important to you is missing from this book please contact us at info@booksumo.com.

We will take your concerns into consideration when the 2nd edition of this book is published. And we will keep you updated!

— BookSumo Press

LEGAL NOTES

COMMON ABBREVIATIONS

cup(s)	C.
tablespoon	tbsp
teaspoon	tsp
ounce	oz.
pound	lb

*All units used are standard American measurements

CHAPTER 1: EASY GRILLING RECIPES

FAJITA FRIDAYS WITH HOMEMADE SALSA

Ingredients

Salsa

- 4 ripe tomatoes, seeded and chopped
- 1 red onion, chopped
- 1 jalapeno pepper, seeded and minced
- 2 tbsp lemon juice, squeezed
- 1 bunch cilantro, chopped
- salt and pepper

Spice Rub

- 2 tbsp paprika
- 2 tsp cumin
- 2 tsp cayenne
- 2 tbsp chili powder
- 2 tsp onion powder
- 2 tsp garlic powder
- 1 tbsp powdered thyme
- 1 tbsp ground marjoram

Fajitas

- 2 lbs. flank steaks
- 2 medium onions, sliced
- 2 -3 bell peppers, sliced
- 2 tbsp olive oil
- 12 (10 inches) flour tortillas
- 1 C. sour cream

Directions

To prepare the salsa:

- Get a mixing bowl: Stir in it all the salsa ingredients.
- Place it in the fridge until ready to serve.

To prepare the spice rub and steak:

- Get a mixing bowl: Stir in it all the spice rub ingredients. Massage it into the steaks.

- Before you do anything, preheat the grill and grease it.
- Cook on it the steaks for 5 to 7 min on each side. Transfer them to a cutting board.
- Let them rest for 5 min then slice them into strips.

To prepare the fajitas:

- Place a large skillet over medium heat. Heat in it the oil.
- Cook in it the pepper and onion slices for 3 to 4 min.
- Heat the tortillas in a pan or microwave. Lay one of them on a cutting board or plate.
- Top it with onion and pepper mix, beef slices, and other toppings of your choice.
- Wrap your tortillas then serve them with your favorite toppings and tomato salsa.
- Enjoy.

Servings Per Recipe: 6

Timing Information:

Preparation	30 mins
Total Time	45 mins

Nutritional Information:

Calories	874.5
Fat	36.7 g
Cholesterol	122.7 mg
Sodium	1061.2 mg
Carbohydrates	88.9 g
Protein	47.5 g

* Percent Daily Values are based on a 2,000 calorie diet.

Masala Chicken

Ingredients

- 3/4 C. plain yogurt
- 1 tbsp tamarind paste
- 3 tbsp garlic, chopped
- 1/4 C. canola oil
- 1 1/2 tsp salt
- 1 1/4 tsp ground cayenne pepper
- 1 tbsp garam masala
- 2 1/4 lbs. boneless chicken thighs
- 1 lemon, cut into 6 wedges

Directions

- Before you do anything else, preheat the grill and grease it.
- Get a mixing bowl: Stir in it the yogurt, tamarind, garlic, canola, salt, cayenne and garam masala.
- Stir in the chicken. Cover the bowl and place it in the fridge overnight.
- Drain the chicken thighs and cook them on the grill for 3 to 4 min on each side.
- Serve them immediately with some lemon wedges.
- Enjoy.

Servings Per Recipe: 4

Timing Information:

Preparation	30 mins
Total Time	8 hrs. 30 mins

Nutritional Information:

Calories	702.9
Fat	54.2 g
Cholesterol	220.4 mg
Sodium	1089.0 mg
Carbohydrates	5.7 g
Protein	46.2 g

* Percent Daily Values are based on a 2,000 calorie diet.

HONEY DIJON KIELBASA

Ingredients

- 3/4-1 lb. beef kielbasa
- 2 tbsp olive oil
- 1 tbsp Dijon mustard
- 1 tbsp prepared horseradish, drained
- 2 tsp white wine vinegar
- 1 tsp honey
- 1/4 tsp salt
- 1/8 tsp pepper
- 1 small Boston lettuce, torn
- 4 crusty bread rolls, halved horizontally

Directions

- Before you do anything, preheat the grill and grease it.
- Slice the smoked kielbasa into 4 pieces. Cut each piece in half lengthwise.
- Get a mixing bowl: Whisk in it the oil, mustard, horseradish, vinegar, honey, salt, and pepper to make the vinaigrette.
- Get a mixing bowl: Stir in it half of the vinaigrette with lettuce. Place it aside.
- Toast the bread rolls for 1 min on each side. Slice them in half and place them on a serving plate.
- Brush the top of the bottom bread halves with the rest of the vinaigrette. Top them with lettuce.
- Grill the sausage pieces for 1 to 2 in on each side. Lay them over the lettuce layer and cover them with the top buns.
- Serve your sandwiches immediately.
- Enjoy.

Servings Per Recipe: 4

Timing Information:

Preparation	15 mins
Total Time	30 mins

Nutritional Information:

Calories	426.4
Fat	24.1 g
Cholesterol	58.8 mg
Sodium	1518.0 mg
Carbohydrates	35.4 g
Protein	16.8 g

* Percent Daily Values are based on a 2,000 calorie diet.

FAJITA SUMMERS

Ingredients

- 1 tbsp paprika
- 1/2 tsp onion salt
- 1/2 tsp garlic powder
- 1/2 tsp ground cayenne pepper
- 1/2 tsp fennel seed, crushed
- 1/2 tsp dried thyme
- 1/4 tsp white pepper
- 1 lb. turkey tenderloins, butterflied
- 1 lime
- 4 pita bread rounds, halved
- 1 C. sour cream
- 1/4 C. green onion, sliced
- 1/4 C. fresh cilantro, chopped
- 1 (4 oz.) cans green chilies, drained
- 1/2 tsp black pepper
- 1/4 tsp cayenne pepper

Directions

- Before you do anything else, preheat the grill and grease it.
- Get a roasting dish: Stir in it the paprika with salt, garlic powder, cayenne pepper, fennel seed, thyme, and pepper.
- Coat the tenderloins with the spice mixture. Cover them with a plastic wrap and refrigerate them for at least 60 min.
- Grill the butterflied tenderloins for 3 to 5 min on each side. Transfer them to a cutting board.
- Drizzle over them the lime then cut them into 1//4 inch strips.
- Get a mixing bowl: Whisk in it the cream with onion, cilantro, chilies, pepper and cayenne pepper to make the sauce.
- Arrange your tenderloin slices in pita halves, with some cream sauce and extra toppings of your choice.
- Enjoy.

Servings Per Recipe: 4

Timing Information:

Preparation	15 mins
Total Time	21 mins

Nutritional Information:

Calories	431.3
Fat	13.2 g
Cholesterol	100.2 mg
Sodium	429.1 mg
Carbohydrates	42.2 g
Protein	35.8 g

* Percent Daily Values are based on a 2,000 calorie diet.

SHRIMP AND SCALLOP PLATTER

Ingredients

- 6 tbsp soy sauce
- 1/4 C. lime juice
- 1/4 C. brown sugar
- 2 tbsp olive oil
- 2 tbsp ketchup
- 3 cloves garlic, minced
- 2 tsp ground coriander
- 1 tsp ground cumin
- 1 lb. shrimp, peeled
- 1 lb. scallops

Directions

- Before you do anything, preheat the grill and grease it.
- Get a mixing bowl: Whisk in it the soy, lime juice, sugar, oil, ketchup, garlic, and spices.
- Add the shrimp with scallops. Toss them to coat.
- Cover the seafood bowl and place it in the fridge for 60 min.
- Drain the shrimp and scallops from the marinade.
- Thread them onto skewers and grill them for 4 to 5 min on each side.
- Serve your seafood skewers warm.
- Enjoy.

Servings Per Recipe: 4

Timing Information:

Preparation	1 hr 20 mins
Total Time	1 hr 28 mins

Nutritional Information:

Calories	367.3
Fat	9.9 g
Cholesterol	210.3 mg
Sodium	1950.4 mg
Carbohydrates	23.2 g
Protein	45.5 g

* Percent Daily Values are based on a 2,000 calorie diet.

HOW TO GRILL VEGETABLES

Ingredients

- 1/4 C. chicken broth
- 1/4 C. balsamic vinegar
- 1 tsp dried oregano
- 1 clove garlic, minced
- 1 tsp olive oil
- 1/4 tsp pepper
- 2 inches sweet onions, sliced
- 2 small sweet red peppers, seeded and chopped
- 2 small zucchini, halved lengthwise
- 1 small eggplant, sliced
- vegetable oil cooking spray

Directions

- Before you do anything else, preheat the grill and grease it.
- Get a mixing bowl: Whisk in it the broth with vinegar, oregano, garlic, oil, and pepper.
- Lay the onion slices in a shallow roasting dish. Top it with pepper, zucchini, and eggplant slices.
- Pour over them half of the broth marinade. Stir them to coat.
- Drain the veggies slices and grill them for 4 to 6 min on each side until they become soft while.
- Baste them while cooking with the remaining broth marinade.
- Serve your grilled veggies immediately.
- Enjoy.

Servings Per Recipe: 4

Timing Information:

Preparation	5 mins
Total Time	40 mins

Nutritional Information:

Calories	82.9
Fat	1.7 g
Cholesterol	0.0 mg
Sodium	59.5 mg
Carbohydrates	15.1 g
Protein	2.9 g

* Percent Daily Values are based on a 2,000 calorie diet.

ACROPOLIS GYROS

Ingredients

- 4 tbsp olive oil
- 2 lbs. Vidalia onions, chopped
- 1 tsp sugar
- 1/4 tsp salt
- 1/4 tsp dried tarragon
- 1/4 tsp dried thyme
- 4 (6 inches) pita bread, halved horizontally
- 6 -7 oz. soft goat cheese, crumbled
- 1 tbsp chopped parsley

Directions

- Before you do anything else, preheat the grill and grease it.
- Place a large pan over medium heat. Heat in it 2 tbsp of oil.
- Stir in it the onions, sugar, and salt. Cook them while stirring for 16 min.
- Lower the heat and let them cook for another 22 min while stirring.
- Get a mixing bowl: Stir in it the 2 tbsp oil, tarragon, and thyme.
- Coat the inside of the pita bread halves with the oil mixture.
- Top them with goat cheese and caramelized onion.
- Lay them on the grill and toast them for 1 to 2 min on each side.
- Once the time is up, serve your pita sandwiches with extra toppings of your choice.
- Enjoy.

Servings Per Recipe: 4

Timing Information:

Preparation	5 mins
Total Time	45 mins

Nutritional Information:

Calories	444.7
Fat	23.2 g
Cholesterol	19.6 mg
Sodium	537.2 mg
Carbohydrates	46.2 g
Protein	14.2 g

* Percent Daily Values are based on a 2,000 calorie diet.

5-Ingredient Chicken Toscano

Ingredients

- 2 chicken breasts
- 1 tomatoes, sliced
- 2 tbsp goat cheese
- 4 -6 basil leaves
- 1 dash pepper

Directions

- Before you do anything, preheat the grill and grease it.
- Use a sharp knife to cut several slits in the chicken breasts.
- Stuff each slit with a tomato slice, basil leaf, and goat cheese while alternating between them.
- Thread the stuffed breasts into toothpicks to seal them. Slice each one of them in half.
- Place the chicken breasts halves on the grill and let them cook for 4 to 6 min on each side until they are done.
- Serve your grilled stuffed chicken warm with your favorite toppings.
- Enjoy.

Servings Per Recipe: 2

Timing Information:

Preparation	5 mins
Total Time	20 mins

Nutritional Information:

Calories	261.7
Fat	13.5 g
Cholesterol	92.8 mg
Sodium	94.6 mg
Carbohydrates	2.5 g
Protein	30.9 g

* Percent Daily Values are based on a 2,000 calorie diet.

North African Grilled Cheeses

Ingredients

- 2 tsp honey
- 1/4 tsp grated lemon rind
- 4 oz. goat cheese
- 8 slices cinnamon raisin bread
- 2 tbsp fig preserves
- 2 tsp basil, sliced
- 1 tbsp margarine
- 1 tsp powdered sugar

Directions

- Get a mixing bowl: Whisk in it the honey, lemon rind, and goat cheese.
- Place 4 bread slices on a serving plate. Spread 1 tbsp of the honey mixture over each slice.
- Top them with 1 1/2 tsp preserves and 1/2 tsp basil. Cover them with the rest of the bread slices.
- Brush the outside of your sandwiches with some butter.
- Preheat the grill and grease it. Grill on it the sandwiches for 1 to min on each side.
- Enjoy.

Servings Per Recipe: 4

Timing Information:

Preparation	6 mins
Total Time	18 mins

Nutritional Information:

Calories	311.5
Fat	13.6 g
Cholesterol	22.4 mg
Sodium	345.5 mg
Carbohydrates	38.2 g
Protein	10.3 g

* Percent Daily Values are based on a 2,000 calorie diet.

Honeymoon Banana Bowls

Ingredients

- 4 ripe bananas, split
- 8 tsp unsalted butter, chopped
- 4 tbsp light brown sugar
- 4 tsp vanilla
- 3 C. vanilla ice cream
- 8 tsp chocolate syrup
- 1/4 C. toasted pecans

Directions

- Before you do anything, preheat the grill and grease it.
- Cut the bananas skin lengthwise open. Slice the banana in half while leaving the skin intact.
- Pull the banana sides open and stuff each one of them with 2 tsp of butter pieces, 1 tbsp brown sugar, and 1 tsp vanilla.
- Place the bananas over the grill and let them cook for 7 to 9 until the butter melts.
- Serve your grilled bananas with ice cream, pecans, and chocolate sauce.
- Enjoy.

Servings Per Recipe: 4

Timing Information:

Preparation	5 mins
Total Time	15 mins

Nutritional Information:

Calories	497.7
Fat	21.0 g
Cholesterol	68.1 mg
Sodium	137.5 mg
Carbohydrates	74.2 g
Protein	5.7 g

* Percent Daily Values are based on a 2,000 calorie diet.

ALASKAN TAILGATE SALMON

Ingredients

- 4 (6 oz.) salmon fillets
- 2 Cedar Planks
- seasoning salt
- black pepper

Topping

- 2 tbsp dill
- 2 tbsp parsley
- 3 tbsp lemon juice
- 2 tbsp oil
- 1/2 tsp black pepper
- white salt

Directions

- Before you do anything, preheat the grill and grease it.
- Soak the cedar planks in water overnight.
- Get a mixing bowl: Whisk in it the dill, parsley, lemon juice, oil and minced fresh garlic to make the sauce.
- Season the salmon fillets with some salt and pepper.
- Place the cedar planks on the grill and put on the lid. Let them cook for 2 to 3 min.
- Place 2 salmon fillets on each plank. Put on the lid and let them cook for 16 to 19 min with the cover on.
- Once the time is up, serve your grilled salmon with dill sauce.
- Enjoy.

Servings Per Recipe: 2

Timing Information:

Preparation	9 hrs.
Total Time	9 hrs. 15 mins

Nutritional Information:

Calories	555.7
Fat	28.5 g
Cholesterol	154.8 mg
Sodium	255.2 mg
Carbohydrates	2.2 g
Protein	69.2 g

* Percent Daily Values are based on a 2,000 calorie diet.

BACKYARD PB & J

Ingredients

- 2 slices whole grain bread
- 2 tsp butter
- 2 tbsp peanut butter
- 1 -2 tbsp jelly

Directions

- Before you do anything, preheat a small grill and grease it.
- Coat one side of each bread slice with 1 tsp of butter.
- Flip them and spoon the peanut butter on one slice and jelly on the other one.
- Flip the bread slice making the peanut butter and jelly sides facing each other.
- Grill the sandwiches for 1 to 2 min on each side then serve them.
- Enjoy.

Servings Per Recipe: 1

Timing Information:

Preparation	5 mins
Total Time	15 mins

Nutritional Information:

Calories	449.5
Fat	25.6 g
Cholesterol	20.1 mg
Sodium	484.4 mg
Carbohydrates	44.0 g
Protein	15.3 g

* Percent Daily Values are based on a 2,000 calorie diet.

MOUNA'S MEDITERREAN LAMB

Ingredients

Marinade

- 2 large garlic cloves, pureed
- 1 tbsp minced rosemary
- 1 pinch cayenne pepper
- 2 tbsp olive oil

Lamb

- 4 shoulder lamb chops
- salt & ground pepper

Directions

- Before you do anything, preheat the grill and grease it.
- Get a mixing bowl: Whisk in it all the marinade ingredients.
- Coat the lamb chops with the marinade and let them sit for 35 min in the fridge.
- Season the chops with some salt and pepper. Grill them for 4 to 6 min on each side.
- Allow your lamb chops to rest for 5 min then serve them.
- Enjoy.

Servings Per Recipe: 4

Timing Information:

Preparation	5 mins
Total Time	40 mins

Nutritional Information:

Calories	63.0
Fat	6.7 g
Cholesterol	0.0 mg
Sodium	0.5 mg
Carbohydrates	0.7 g
Protein	0.1 g

* Percent Daily Values are based on a 2,000 calorie diet.

BLACKENED BEETS

Ingredients

- 2 lbs. beets, peeled and quartered
- 2 tbsp olive oil
- 2 tsp sea salt
- 1/4 tsp ground black pepper

Directions

- Before you do anything, preheat the grill and grease it.
- Sprinkle some salt and pepper all over the beet quarters.
- Grill them for 5 to 8 min until they become soft. Serve them warm with some sour cream.
- Enjoy.

Servings Per Recipe: 6

Timing Information:

Preparation	10 mins
Total Time	30 mins

Nutritional Information:

Calories	106.7
Fat	4.7 g
Cholesterol	0.0 mg
Sodium	891.9 mg
Carbohydrates	15.1 g
Protein	2.5 g

* Percent Daily Values are based on a 2,000 calorie diet.

SOUTH AMERICAN BLACK BEAN CHICKEN BREASTS

Ingredients

- 4 boneless skinless chicken breasts
- 3 tbsp lime juice
- 1 tbsp vegetable oil
- 1/4 tsp crushed red pepper flakes
- 3 garlic cloves, crushed
- 1 C. water
- 1/2 C. red bell pepper, diced
- 1 tbsp red onion, chopped

Sauce

- 1 C. black beans, drained
- 1/2 C. orange juice
- 2 tbsp balsamic vinegar
- 1/4 tsp salt
- 1/8 tsp black pepper
- 1 garlic clove, crushed

Directions

To prepare the grilled chicken:

- Get a large mixing bowl: Whisk in it the lime juice, vegetable oil, red pepper, and garlic.
- Add to it the chicken breasts and coat them with the marinade.
- Cover the bowl with a plastic wrap and refrigerate it overnight.
- Place saucepan of water over high heat. Heat it until it starts boiling.
- Blanch in it the onion with bell pepper for 40 sec. Drain them and place them in a bowl of ice water.
- Drain them immediately and place them aside.
- Before you do anything else, preheat the grill and grease it.
- Drain the chicken breasts from the marinade. Grill them for 9 to 12 min on each side.
- Cover them with a piece of foil and let them rest for 4 to 5 min.

To prepare the bean sauce:

- Get a blender: Combine in it all the bean sauce ingredients. Blend them smooth.
- Pour the sauce into a small saucepan. Heat it for few minutes then serve it with the grilled chicken, onion and pepper.
- Enjoy.

Servings Per Recipe: 4

Timing Information:

Preparation	1 hr
Total Time	1 hr

Nutritional Information:

Calories	256.7
Fat	6.8 g
Cholesterol	75.5 mg
Sodium	288.2 mg
Carbohydrates	18.1 g
Protein	29.5 g

* Percent Daily Values are based on a 2,000 calorie diet.

PACIFIC SHRIMP WITH POLYNESIAN SALSA

Ingredients

Salsa

- 1 1/2 C. canned crushed pineapple, drained
- 1 jalapeno pepper, seeded and chopped
- 1 red bell pepper, seeded and diced
- 2 tbsp lime juice
- salt

Shrimp

- 1/2 C. light coconut milk
- 2 tbsp lime juice
- 1 tbsp low sodium soy sauce
- 1 tbsp grated gingerroot
- 1 tbsp brown sugar
- 20 large shrimp, peeled and deveined
- fresh ground black pepper
- 3 C. cooked rice
- 1/2 C. cilantro, sprigs
- 4 metal skewers

Directions

To prepare the pineapple salsa:

- Get a mixing bowl: Stir in it all the salsa ingredients.
- Place it in the fridge until ready to serve.

To prepare the grilled shrimp:

- Get a mixing bowl: Whisk in it the coconut milk, lime juice, soy sauce, ginger and brown sugar. Stir in the shrimp with a pinch of salt and pepper. Cover it and place it in the fridge for 60 min.
- Once the time is up, preheat the grill and grease it.
- Drain the shrimp pieces from the marinade and thread them onto wooden skewers. Grill them for 4 to 5 min on each side.
- Serve your grilled shrimp warm with the chilled pineapple salsa.
- Enjoy.

Servings Per Recipe: 4

Timing Information:

Preparation	8 hrs.
Total Time	8 hrs. 8 mins

Nutritional Information:

Calories	267.6
Fat	0.8 g
Cholesterol	53.6 mg
Sodium	215.8 mg
Carbohydrates	54.8 g
Protein	10.1 g

* Percent Daily Values are based on a 2,000 calorie diet.

CHIPOTLE MANGOES

Ingredients

- 2 mangoes, ripe but firm
- 2 tbsp lime juice
- 2 tsp chili powder
- 1 tsp salt

Directions

- Before you do anything, preheat the grill and grease it.
- Peel and slice the mangos in half. Grill them for 3 to 4 min on each side.
- Arrange the mangos on a serving plate. Drizzle over them the lime juice with chili powder and salt.
- Serve them immediately.
- Enjoy.

Servings Per Recipe: 4

Timing Information:

Preparation	12 mins
Total Time	13 mins

Nutritional Information:

Calories	106.5
Fat	0.8 g
Cholesterol	0.0 mg
Sodium	605.3 mg
Carbohydrates	26.4 g
Protein	1.5 g

* Percent Daily Values are based on a 2,000 calorie diet.

HOT MAHI MAHI

Ingredients

Salsa

- 1 ripe avocado, peeled and cubed
- 2 Roma tomatoes, diced
- 1 C. minced red onion
- 1 jalapeno pepper, minced
- 1/2 C. cilantro
- 1 lime, juice
- 1/2 tsp kosher salt

Mahi Mahi

- 3 lbs. mahi-mahi, cut into 6 pieces
- 1 tbsp extra virgin olive oil
- 1 lime, juice
- 1/2 tsp kosher salt

Directions

To prepare the salsa:

- Get a mixing bowl: Stir in it all the salsa ingredients.
- Chill it in the fridge until ready to serve.

To prepare the grilled mahi-mahi:

- Get a mixing bowl: Whisk in it the olive oil, lime, salt, and pepper.
- Add to it the fish strips and toss them to coat.
- Cover them and chill them in the fridge for 25 to 35 min.
- Before you do anything, preheat the grill and grease it.
- Drain the fish strips from the marinade and grill them for 7 to 9 min on each side.
- Serve your grilled fish with avocado salsa.
- Enjoy.

Servings Per Recipe: 6

Timing Information:

Preparation	15 mins
Total Time	27 mins

Nutritional Information:

Calories	285.1
Fat	8.8 g
Cholesterol	165.4 mg
Sodium	592.5 mg
Carbohydrates	7.5 g
Protein	43.1 g

* Percent Daily Values are based on a 2,000 calorie diet.

SEATTLE POTATO SALAD

Ingredients

- 2 quarts water, salted
- 2 lbs. baby new potatoes, assorted
- 1 lb. French style green bean, trimmed
- olive oil flavored cooking spray
- 1 garlic clove, peeled and minced
- 1 tbsp Dijon mustard
- 1 tbsp balsamic vinegar
- 1/2 C. fresh parsley, chopped
- 1 tbsp of fresh mint, chopped
- 1 tbsp extra virgin olive oil
- salt and pepper
- 1 C. kalamata olive, pitted, herbed
- 1-pint cherry tomatoes, halved

Directions

- Bring a salted pot of water to a boil. Cook in it the potatoes for 4 to 6 min until they become soft.
- Drain the potatoes and pat them dry. Slice them in half.
- Stir the beans into the same pot and cook them for 5 min. Drain them and place them in a bowl of ice-cold water.
- Drain it and place it aside.
- Before you do anything, preheat the grill and grease it.
- Coat the potato halves with some olive oil or a cooking spray. Grill them for 2 to 3 min on each side.
- Get a large mixing bowl: Combine in it the garlic, mustard, vinegar, parsley, and mint.
- Add the olive oil gradually while whisking all the time.
- Add the grilled potatoes with a pinch of salt and pepper. Toss them to coat.
- Stir in the tomato with olives and beans.
- Adjust the seasoning of your salad then serve it.
- Enjoy.

Servings Per Recipe: 4

Timing Information:

Preparation	35 mins
Total Time	35 mins

Nutritional Information:

Calories	243.3
Fat	3.9 g
Cholesterol	0.0 mg
Sodium	348.0 mg
Carbohydrates	48.1 g
Protein	6.7 g

* Percent Daily Values are based on a 2,000 calorie diet.

BLACKENED PINEAPPLE

Ingredients

- 1 ripe pineapple, peeled, cored and cut into wedges
- 1/2 C. melted unsalted butter
- 3/4 C. granulated sugar
- 1 tsp ground cinnamon
- 1/8 tsp ground cloves
- 1-pint vanilla ice cream

Directions

- Before you do anything, preheat the grill and grease it.
- Get a shallow roasting dish: Pour in it the melted butter.
- Get a mixing bowl: Stir in it the sugar, cinnamon, and cloves.
- Coat the pineapple wedges with melted butter then roll them in the sugar mix.
- Place them on the grill and cook them for 6 to 9 min on each side.
- Serve your grilled pineapple with some vanilla ice cream.
- Enjoy.

Servings Per Recipe: 8

Timing Information:

Preparation	10 mins
Total Time	25 mins

Nutritional Information:

Calories	275.2
Fat	15.5 g
Cholesterol	46.2 mg
Sodium	30.8 mg
Carbohydrates	34.8 g
Protein	1.7 g

* Percent Daily Values are based on a 2,000 calorie diet.

GARDEN COUSCOUS

Ingredients

Shrimp

- 1 lb. cleaned and peeled grilled shrimp
- 1 tsp olive oil
- 1 tsp soy sauce
- 1 tbsp marmalade

Couscous

- 2 tbsp olive oil
- 1/4 C. sweet onion
- 1 clove garlic, minced

- 1/4 inch fresh ginger, minced
- 2 tbsp Worcestershire sauce
- 1 C. chicken broth
- 1 C. passion fruit
- 2/3 C. citrus marmalade
- 1/2 lb. couscous
- 1 dash cayenne pepper
- 1 tsp grated orange zest
- 1/2 C. dry roasted macadamias, crushed
- 1/4 C. dried cranberries
- 3 tbsp chopped parsley
- salt and pepper

Directions

- Before you do anything, preheat the grill and grease it.
- Get a mixing bowl: Toss in it the shrimp with olive oil, soy sauce, marmalade, a pinch of salt and pepper. Cover the bowl and let it sit for 16 min. Drain the shrimp and thread them onto skewers. Grill them for 3 to 4 min on each side.
- Place a heavy saucepan over medium heat. Heat in it the olive oil.
- Cook in it the onion, ginger, and garlic for 3 min.
- Add the stock with Worcestershire sauce, juice marmalade, and cayenne pepper. Mix them well. Cook them until they start boiling. Stir in the couscous with orange zest. Turn off the heat and put on the lid. Let them sit for 10 to 12 min. Once the time is up, add the nuts, dried cranberries, herbs, and shrimp. Mix them with a fork. Serve your grilled shrimp couscous warm. Enjoy.

Servings Per Recipe: 8

Timing Information:

Preparation	15 mins
Total Time	25 mins

Nutritional Information:

Calories	371.0
Fat	11.4 g
Cholesterol	110.4 mg
Sodium	334.8 mg
Carbohydrates	51.5 g
Protein	17.6 g

* Percent Daily Values are based on a 2,000 calorie diet.

CALIFORNIA TOPPED TOFU

Ingredients

- 2 packages firm tofu, drained
- 2 Texas starred grapefruits
- 3 navel oranges
- 4 tsp olive oil
- 3/4 tsp cayenne pepper
- 1/4 tsp salt, divided
- 1/2 red bell pepper, seeded and minced
- 1/4 red onion, minced
- 2 tbsp fresh cilantro, minced and packed
- 1 bag Florentine Baby Spinach, washed and dried
- 1/2 avocado, ripe but firm, diced

Directions

To prepare the tofu:

- Slice the tofu block then cut each slice into 2 pieces making two triangles.
- Get a mixing bowl: Whisk in it the juice of half grapefruit with the juice of half an orange, and 1 tbsp of oil.
- Pat the tofu slices dry then arrange them in a roasting dish.
- Pour over them the juice mixture. Layover it a plastic wrap to cover it. Let it sit overnight in the fridge.

To prepare the salsa:

- Peel and cut the remaining grapefruits and oranges into segments.
- Get a mixing bowl: Stir in it the fruit segments with bell pepper, red onion, cilantro and a pinch of salt.
- Place it in the fridge until ready to serve.
- Place a grilling pan over medium heat. Heat in it 1 tsp of olive oil.

- Stir in it the tofu with its marinade. Let them cook for 3 to 4 min on each side.
- Once the time is up, drain them and transfer them to a serving plate.
- Stir the spinach into the same pan and cook them for 2 min.
- Transfer the spinach into serving plates followed by tofu slices and fruit salsa.
- Enjoy.

Servings Per Recipe: 4

Timing Information:

Preparation	3 hrs.
Total Time	3 hrs. 20 mins

Nutritional Information:

Calories	207.9
Fat	8.9 g
Cholesterol	0.0 mg
Sodium	205.5 mg
Carbohydrates	32.7 g
Protein	4.7 g

* Percent Daily Values are based on a 2,000 calorie diet.

Dad's Favorite

(Whole Leg of Lamb)

Ingredients

- 7 -8 lbs. leg of lamb, trimmed of all fat, boned
- 1 lemon

Rub

- 8 cloves garlic, chopped
- 2 tbsp chopped thyme leaves
- 2 tbsp chopped rosemary leaves
- 2 tbsp chopped parsley leaves
- 1/2 tsp ground black pepper
- 1 tbsp coarse salt
- 3 tbsp olive oil

Directions

- Before you do anything else, preheat the grill and grease it.
- Get a mixing bowl: Mix in it the garlic with thyme, rosemary, parsley, pepper, salt and olive oil.
- Coat the lamb leg with the rub mixture. Let it sit in the fridge for 60 min.
- Grill in it the lamb leg for 12 to 14 min on each side.
- Serve it warm with some lemon wedges.
- Enjoy.

Servings Per Recipe: 8

Timing Information:

Preparation	20 mins
Total Time	40 mins

Nutritional Information:

Calories	850.9
Fat	58.6 g
Cholesterol	265.9 mg
Sodium	1099.7 mg
Carbohydrates	2.0 g
Protein	74.1 g

* Percent Daily Values are based on a 2,000 calorie diet.

SOUTHWEST TORTILLA SOUP

Ingredients

- 3 skinless, boneless chicken breast halves
- 8 C. water
- 8 tsp chicken bouillon granules
- 1 C. chopped carrot
- 1/4 tsp ground allspice
- 1/2 tsp chopped fresh thyme
- 1/8 tsp ground cinnamon
- 1 tbsp chopped fresh ginger
- 1 tbsp minced garlic
- 1 C. chopped tomato
- 1 C. coconut milk
- 1 tsp hot pepper sauce
- 1 C. mozzarella cheese, grated
- 2 C. crispy tortilla strips
- 2 limes, cut into wedges

Directions

- Before you do anything preheat the grill and grease it.
- Season the chicken breasts with some salt and pepper. Cook them on the grill for 7 to 9 min on each side.
- Place the chicken breasts aside and allow them to cool down for a while. Slice them into chunks and transfer them to a large pot.
- Add to them the water, bouillon and carrot, allspice, thyme, cinnamon, ginger and garlic. Cook them until they start boiling over high medium heat.
- Lower the heat and cook the soup for 12 min. Add the tomato, coconut milk and hot pepper sauce. Let the soup cook for an extra 2 to 3 min.
- Once the time is up, serve your soup hot with some mozzarella cheese, tortilla strips and lime wedges.
- Enjoy.

Servings per Recipe: 8

Timing Information:

Preparation	20 m
Cooking	20 m
Total Time	40 m

Nutritional Information:

Calories	196
Fat	11.3
Carbohydrates	35
Protein	540
Cholesterol	10.6
Sodium	14.6

* Percent Daily Values are based on a 2,000 calorie diet.

POLYNESIAN SUNSET SKEWERS

Ingredients

- 1 lb. uncooked jumbo shrimp
- 1/2 fresh pineapple, peeled, cored and diced
- 6 tbsp orange marmalade, divided
- 1/2 C. water
- 1 tbsp soy sauce
- couple dashes hot sauce
- 1 (6 oz.) boxes long grain and wild rice blend
- 1/4 C. snipped cilantro

Directions

- Before you do anything, preheat the grill and grease it.
- Place a heavy saucepan over medium heat. Stir in it 4 tbsp of the marmalade, water, soy sauce and hot sauce.
- Heat them for 1 to 2 min then turn off the heat.
- Thread the shrimp pieces and pineapple dices onto skewers while alternating between them.
- Coat them with the marmalade sauce and grill them for 10 to 12 min. Serve them warm.
- Enjoy.

Servings Per Recipe: 4

Timing Information:

Preparation	30 mins
Total Time	40 mins

Nutritional Information:

Calories	213.8
Fat	1.2 g
Cholesterol	143.0 mg
Sodium	913.0 mg
Carbohydrates	36.0 g
Protein	16.6 g

* Percent Daily Values are based on a 2,000 calorie diet.

BACKYARD BAHN MI

Ingredients

- 1 tbsp garlic, minced
- 1 tbsp fish sauce
- 1 tbsp soy sauce
- 1 tsp sugar
- 1/2 tsp ground black pepper
- 2 tbsp peanut oil
- 1 lb. sirloin, sliced
- 5 shallots, sliced
- 4 French baguettes
- 8 lettuce leaves
- 1 C. carrot
- 4 sprigs cilantro

Directions

- Get a mixing bowl: Whisk in it the garlic, fish sauce, soy sauce, sugar, pepper, and 1 tbsp peanut oil.
- Stir in the beef slices. Cover the bowl and place it in the fridge for 30 min.
- Place a grill pan over medium heat. Heat in it 1 tbsp of oil.
- Cook in it the beef slices in batches for 1 min on each side.
- Cut the Frenchh baguettes in half.
- Lay in them the lettuce leaves followed by beef slices, carrot, shallot, and cilantro.
- Serve your sandwiches immediately with extra toppings of your choice.
- Enjoy.

Servings Per Recipe: 4

Timing Information:

Preparation	20 mins
Total Time	30 mins

Nutritional Information:

Calories	1609.0
Fat	38.9 g
Cholesterol	75.9 mg
Sodium	3458.2 mg
Carbohydrates	246.0 g
Protein	63.9 g

* Percent Daily Values are based on a 2,000 calorie diet.

STRIP STEAK MARRAKECH

Ingredients

- 1 tsp ground allspice
- 1 tsp ground cumin
- 1 tsp ground ginger
- 1 tsp kosher salt
- 1/2 tsp ground cinnamon
- 1/2 tsp ground coriander
- 1/2 tsp cayenne pepper
- 1 lb. strips steak, trimmed of visible fat and cut into 4 portions
- 2 medium sweet potatoes
- 1 medium red onion, halved and sliced
- 4 tsp canola oil
- 1 tsp grated orange zest

Directions

- Before you do anything, preheat the grill and grease it.
- Get a mixing bowl: Mix in it the allspice, cumin, ginger, salt, cinnamon, coriander, and cayenne.
- Coat the steaks with 4 1/2 tsp of the spice mixture. Place them aside.
- Get a large mixing bowl: Combine in it the remaining spice mixture with sweet potatoes, onion, and canola oil.
- Stir them to coat. Spoon half of the mix to a large piece of foil then fold it around it in the shape of a packet.
- Repeat the process with the other half.
- Place the steaks and potato packets over the grill. Grill them for 5 to 6 min on each side.
- Serve them both warm.
- Enjoy.

Servings Per Recipe: 4

Timing Information:

Preparation	10 mins
Total Time	35 mins

Nutritional Information:

Calories	398.1
Fat	26.4 g
Cholesterol	77.1 mg
Sodium	534.3 mg
Carbohydrates	17.3 g
Protein	22.1 g

* Percent Daily Values are based on a 2,000 calorie diet.

RUSTY'S FAVORITE SEAFOOD SAMPLER

Ingredients

- 12 large shrimp
- 20 large sea scallops
- 1 green pepper
- 1 large Spanish onion
- 16 medium mushrooms, whole

- 2 garlic cloves, minced
- 1/4 C. lemon juice
- 1/2 tsp sea salt
- 1/4 tsp black pepper, ground
- 3/4 C. olive oil
- 1/4 lb. butter, melted
- 4 tbsp honey

Marinade

- 4 tbsp ginger, minced

Directions

- Before you do anything, preheat the grill and grease it.
- Get a mixing bowl: Whisk in it all the marinade ingredients.
- Get a large mixing bowl: Stir in it 1/3 of the marinade with shrimp and scallops.
- Cover them and place the bowl in the fridge for at least 120 min.
- Get a large mixing bowl: Stir in it 1/4 of the remaining marinade with onion and mushrooms.
- Let them sit for 35 min to marinate.
- Thread the shrimp, scallops, onion, and mushrooms onto skewers while alternating between them.
- Grill them for 3 to 5 min while turning them. Serve them warm.
- Enjoy.

Servings Per Recipe: 4

Timing Information:

Preparation	20 mins
Total Time	30 mins

Nutritional Information:

Calories	737.3
Fat	64.4 g
Cholesterol	101.6 mg
Sodium	898.0 mg
Carbohydrates	29.8 g
Protein	14.9 g

* Percent Daily Values are based on a 2,000 calorie diet.

GRILLED ONIONS FOR EVERYTHING

Ingredients

- 2 large sweet onions, peeled
- 2 tbsp butter, melted
- 2 tsp honey
- 2 tsp dry mustard

Directions

- Get a mixing bowl: Whisk in it the butter with mustard and honey.
- Get a large piece of foil. Fold it in half.
- Place in the center of it the onions. Drizzle over them the butter mixture.
- Bring the sides of the foil over the onion then pinch them to seal them.
- Place them on the grill and let them cook for 30 to 35 min. Serve them warm.
- Enjoy.

Servings Per Recipe: 1

Timing Information:

Preparation	5 mins
Total Time	35 mins

Nutritional Information:

Calories	201.3
Fat	12.5 g
Cholesterol	30.5 mg
Sodium	86.7 mg
Carbohydrates	22.0 g
Protein	2.3 g

* Percent Daily Values are based on a 2,000 calorie diet.

6-Ingredient Yaktori

Ingredients

- 1/2 C. light soy sauce
- 1/4 C. apple juice
- 2 tbsp brown sugar
- 2 tsp grated ginger
- 1 tsp minced garlic
- 4 boneless chicken breasts

Directions

- Before you do anything, preheat the grill and grease it.
- Get a mixing bowl: Whisk in it the soy sauce with apple juice, sugar, ginger, and garlic.
- Poke the chicken breasts with a skewer several times.
- Place them in a large bowl and cover them with the marinade.
- Cover the bowl and place it in the fridge for at least 4 h.
- Drain the chicken breasts and grill them for 6 to 8 min on each side. Serve them warm.
- Enjoy.

Servings Per Recipe: 4

Timing Information:

Preparation	5 mins
Total Time	15 mins

Nutritional Information:

Calories	308.9
Fat	13.5 g
Cholesterol	92.8 mg
Sodium	2146.0 mg
Carbohydrates	11.4 g
Protein	34.2 g

* Percent Daily Values are based on a 2,000 calorie diet.

POPCORN PEPPERS

Ingredients

- 1/4 C. sour cream
- 16 miniature sweet peppers
- 1 C. shredded Mexican blend cheese
- 1 tomatoes, cored, seeded, and diced
- 1/4 C. red onion, diced
- 1/4 C. cilantro, chopped
- 1/2 tsp sea salt

Directions

- Before you do anything, preheat the grill and grease it.
- Pour the sour cream into a large zip lock bag. Place it in the fridge to chill.
- Slice the peppers in halves then discard their seeds and veins.
- Get a mixing bowl: Combine in it the cheese, tomato, onion, cilantro, and salt.
- Spoon the mixture into the pepper halves and press it down.
- Grill them with the cheese side facing up for 4 to 6 min. Transfer them to a serving plate.
- Snip the tip of the sour cream bag then drizzle it over the grilled peppers.
- Serve them right away.
- Enjoy.

Servings Per Recipe: 6

Timing Information:

Preparation	25 mins
Total Time	28 mins

Nutritional Information:

Calories	191.7
Fat	9.6 g
Cholesterol	27.3 mg
Sodium	455.5 mg
Carbohydrates	22.0 g
Protein	8.4 g

* Percent Daily Values are based on a 2,000 calorie diet.

THAI STYLE CORN

Ingredients

- 4 tbsp butter
- 1 tbsp hoisin sauce
- 2 1/2 tsp grated orange peel
- 3/4 tsp chili-garlic sauce
- 6 ears white corn, husked, and rinsed
- chopped cilantro

Directions

- Before you do anything, preheat the grill and grease it.
- Get a mixing bowl: Mix in it the butter with hoisin sauce, orange peel, garlic sauce, a pinch of salt and pepper.
- Place the ears of corn over the grill and cook them for 5 to 6 min while turning them.
- Coat them with the butter sauce mixture then grill them for another 5 to 6 min.
- Garnish your grilled corn with some cilantro then serve them warm.
- Enjoy.

Servings Per Recipe: 6

Timing Information:

Preparation	20 mins
Total Time	20 mins

Nutritional Information:

Calories	151.9
Fat	8.8 g
Cholesterol	20.4 mg
Sodium	124.1 mg
Carbohydrates	18.5 g
Protein	3.0 g

* Percent Daily Values are based on a 2,000 calorie diet.

FRUITY CHICKEN SALAD

Ingredients

- 2 -3 chicken breasts
- 1/2 C. raspberry vinaigrette dressing
- 1/2 tsp garlic powder
- 1/2 tsp rosemary
- 4 C. lettuce, torn
- 1 C. cucumber, sliced
- 1/2 C. mandarin orange, drained
- 1/2 C. raspberries
- 1/4 C. red onion, chopped
- 1/2 C. pecans, chopped
- additional raspberry vinaigrette dressing

Directions

- Before you do anything, preheat the grill and grease it.
- Get a mixing bowl: Whisk in it 1/2 C. dressing with garlic powder and rosemary.
- Add the chicken breasts and toss them to coat. Cover the bowl and chill it in the fridge for 1 h to overnight.
- Drain the chicken breasts and grill them for 5 to 7 min on each side. Serve them warm.
- Enjoy.

Servings Per Recipe: 4

Timing Information:

Preparation	10 mins
Total Time	10 mins

Nutritional Information:

Calories	254.4
Fat	16.7 g
Cholesterol	46.4 mg
Sodium	57.5 mg
Carbohydrates	10.1 g
Protein	17.5 g

* Percent Daily Values are based on a 2,000 calorie diet.

GINGER SESAME CHICKEN AND NOODLES

Ingredients

- 3 lbs. bone-in chicken breasts

Marinade

- 2 tbsp rice vinegar
- 2 tbsp low sodium soy sauce
- 1 tsp dark sesame oil
- 1 tsp grated ginger

Sauce

- 1/4 C. hoisin sauce

- 1/4 C. ketchup
- 2 tbsp low sodium soy sauce
- 2 tbsp honey
- 1 tsp grated ginger
- 1 tsp dark sesame oil

Garnish

- 1 tbsp toasted sesame seeds
- 2 -3 C. uncooked mai fun rice noodles
- cooking oil

Directions

- Before you do anything, preheat the grill and grease it.
- Get a mixing bowl: Whisk in it all the marinade ingredients.
- Add to it the chicken breasts and stir them to coat. Cover the bowl and refrigerate it overnight.
- Place a deep pan over medium heat. Heat in it 2 inches of oil.
- Place in it some of the mai noodles and fry it until it floats on top.
- Drain it immediately and place it on paper towels to drain.
- Repeat the process with the remaining noodles.

To prepare the glaze sauce:

- Place a heavy saucepan over medium heat. Stir in it all the sauce ingredients.

- Heat them until they start boiling. Lower the heat and let it cook for 4 min.
- Once the time is up, turn off the heat and let it lose heat completely.

To prepare the basting marinade:

- Drain the chicken breasts and place them aside. Pour the marinade into a heavy saucepan.
- Heat them until they start boiling. Lower the heat and let them cook for 3 min.
- Turn off the heat and let it lose heat completely.
- Grill the chicken breasts for 50 to 75 min overall while basting them with marinade.
- Once the time is up, coat them with the glaze sauce. Grill them for few more minutes until they become sticky.
- Arrange the noodles between serving plates. Top them with the chicken breasts then serve them warm.
- Enjoy.

Servings Per Recipe: 3

Timing Information:

| Preparation | 24 hrs. |
| Total Time | 25 hrs. 15 mins |

Nutritional Information:

Calories	959.8
Fat	48.1 g
Cholesterol	291.2 mg
Sodium	1654.7 mg
Carbohydrates	30.0 g
Protein	97.9 g

* Percent Daily Values are based on a 2,000 calorie diet.

ASHLEIGH'S HOT JAMAICAN CHICKEN

Ingredients

- 1 large red onion
- 3 cloves garlic
- 1 habanero pepper, seeded
- 1 tbsp fresh ginger root
- 1/4 C. olive oil
- 1/4 C. brown sugar
- 3 tbsp red wine vinegar
- 3 tbsp orange juice concentrate, thawed
- 1 tsp soy sauce
- 2 tsp ground cinnamon
- 1/2 tsp ground nutmeg
- 1/4 tsp ground cloves
- 1/2 C. chopped cilantro
- 1/2 tsp salt and pepper to taste
- 6 skinless, boneless chicken breast halves

Directions

- Get a food processor: Combine in it the onion, garlic, habanero pepper, and ginger. Process them until they become smooth.
- Add the olive oil, brown sugar, vinegar, orange juice concentrate, soy sauce, cinnamon, nutmeg, cloves, cilantro, salt, and pepper. Blend them smooth again.
- Get a large mixing bowl: Place in it the chicken breasts and pour the marinade all over it. Stir them well to coat.
- Cover the bowl with a plastic wrap. Place it in the fridge for an overnight.
- Before you do anything else, preheat the grill and grease it.
- Drain the chicken breasts from the marinade and cook them for 10 to 12 min on each or until they are done to your liking.
- Serve your grilled chicken breasts with your favorite salad.
- Enjoy.

Servings per Recipe: 6

Timing Information:

Preparation	30 m
Cooking	30 m
Total Time	1 d 1 h

Nutritional Information:

Calories	279
Fat	12
Carbohydrates	67
Protein	309
Cholesterol	17
Sodium	25.3

* Percent Daily Values are based on a 2,000 calorie diet.

Honey Dijon Onions

Ingredients

- 1 red onion, sliced
- 1 yellow onion, sliced
- 1 tbsp olive oil
- 2 tbsp honey
- 1 tsp rosemary, chopped
- 1 tsp Dijon mustard

Directions

- Before you do anything, preheat the grill and grease it.
- Get a mixing bowl: Whisk in it the oil, honey, rosemary and Dijon mustard.
- Coat the onion slices with the honey mixture.
- Grill them for 3 to 4 min until they become soft. Serve them warm.
- Enjoy.

Servings Per Recipe: 4

Timing Information:

Preparation	5 mins
Total Time	13 mins

Nutritional Information:

Calories	85.9
Fat	3.4 g
Cholesterol	0.0 mg
Sodium	16.1 mg
Carbohydrates	14.3 g
Protein	0.5 g

* Percent Daily Values are based on a 2,000 calorie diet.

POTATO SALAD SUMMERS

Ingredients

- 5 medium potatoes
- 1/2 C. mayonnaise
- 1/4 C. white vinegar
- 2 tsp sugar
- 1 tsp salt
- 1 tsp dry mustard
- 1/4 tsp ground black pepper
- 8 slices cooked turkey bacon, crumbled
- 1 C. chopped celery
- 1/3 C. chopped green onion

Directions

- Before you do anything, preheat the grill and grease it.
- Place a large saucepan of salted water over high heat.
- Add to it the potatoes and heat it until it starts boiling. Let them cook until they become soft.
- Get a mixing bowl: Whisk in it the mayonnaise, vinegar, sugar, salt, mustard, and pepper.
- Stir in the potatoes, bacon, celery, and onion.
- Get a large piece of foil. Fold it in half. Pour in the middle of it the potato mixture.
- Pull the foil over the mixture and pinch it to seal it.
- Grill it for 10 min on each side. Serve it warm.
- Enjoy.

Servings Per Recipe: 4

Timing Information:

Preparation	20 mins
Total Time	40 mins

Nutritional Information:

Calories	427.8
Fat	17.0 g
Cholesterol	25.2 mg
Sodium	1198.1 mg
Carbohydrates	57.7 g
Protein	12.1 g

* Percent Daily Values are based on a 2,000 calorie diet.

GRILLED CHICKEN QUARTERS

Ingredients

- 1 whole chicken, quartered lengthwise
- 2 limes, juice
- 1/2 C. olive oil
- 1 onion, minced
- 1/2 tsp saffron
- salt and pepper

Directions

- Before you do anything, preheat the grill and grease it.
- Get a mixing bowl: Stir in it all the ingredients.
- Cover the bowl and let it marinate for at least 1 h.
- Drain the chicken pieces from the marinade. Grill them for 12 to 16 min on each side.
- Serve them warm with some grilled veggies.
- Enjoy.

Servings Per Recipe: 4

Timing Information:

Preparation	10 mins
Total Time	40 mins

Nutritional Information:

Calories	
Fat	413.6
Cholesterol	38.6 g
Sodium	53.4 mg
Carbohydrates	52.0 mg
Protein	4.4 g

* Percent Daily Values are based on a 2,000 calorie diet.

Pizza Mexicana

Ingredients

- pizza dough
- 2 tbsp cornmeal
- 1 tsp olive oil
- 18 large shrimp, peeled and deveined
- 1/8 tsp salt
- 1 C. shredded part-skim mozzarella cheese
- 1 C. queso fresco, crumbled
- 3 tbsp salsa verde
- 1/4 C. cilantro leaves

Directions

- Before you do anything, preheat the grill and grease it.
- Get a mixing bowl: Stir in it all the cheeses.
- Press the shrimp onto skewers.
- Season them with a pinch of salt then spray them with a cooking spray.
- Grill them for 2 to 3 min on each side. Let it lose heat for a while then chop it.
- Sprinkle some cornmeal in a baking sheet. Layover it the dough.
- Coat it with olive oil. Slide it over the grill and let it cook for 3 to 4 min.
- Flip the pizza crust and top it with salsa leaving the sides empty.
- Sprinkle the chopped shrimp and cheese on top. Let the pizza cook 3 to 4 min.
- Garnish it with cilantro then serve it right away.
- Enjoy.

Servings Per Recipe: 4

Timing Information:

Preparation	10 mins
Total Time	16 mins

Nutritional Information:

Calories	197.7
Fat	10.7 g
Cholesterol	88.5 mg
Sodium	660.4 mg
Carbohydrates	4.9 g
Protein	19.7 g

* Percent Daily Values are based on a 2,000 calorie diet.

FLAMED ONIONS

Ingredients

- 2 large sweet red onions
- 12 slices turkey bacon, sliced into strips
- 1/2 C. packed brown sugar
- 1/2 C. balsamic vinegar
- 1/4 C. molasses
- 2 tbsp barbecue sauce
- ground pepper

Directions

- Before you do anything else, preheat the grill and grease it.
- Slice each onion into 12 wedges.
- Lay a strip of bacon over each onion wedge and wrap it. Secure it with a toothpick.
- Repeat the process with the remaining onion and bacon strips.
- Get a mixing bowl: Whisk in it the brown sugar, vinegar, molasses, fresh ground pepper and barbecue sauce.
- Place the onion and bacon skewers in a roasting dish. Pour half of the vinegar marinade all over them.
- Layover it a plastic wrap to cover it. Chill it in the fridge for 60 min while turning the skewers halfway through.
- Drain the onion and bacon skewers.
- Grill them for 8 to 9 min on each side while basting them with the remaining marinade.
- Enjoy.

Servings Per Recipe: 1

Timing Information:

Preparation	20 mins
Total Time	30 mins

Nutritional Information:

Calories	1069.5
Fat	61.8 g
Cholesterol	92.4 mg
Sodium	1318.6 mg
Carbohydrates	112.8 g
Protein	18.6 g

* Percent Daily Values are based on a 2,000 calorie diet.

6-INGREDIENT POTATO SKEWERS

Ingredients

- 4 lbs. tiny new potatoes
- salt
- 1/3 C. olive oil
- 2 tsp minced garlic
- 1/2 tsp dried thyme
- 1/2 tsp black pepper

Directions

- Before you do anything, preheat the grill and grease it.
- Place a large saucepan of salted water over high heat.
- Cook in it the potatoes for 10 to 14 min until they become soft.
- Once the time is up, drain them and transfer them to a mixing bowl.
- Add the oil with garlic, thyme, and pepper. Toss them to coat.
- Place the potatoes over the grill and cook them for 10 min while turning them.
- Serve your grilled potatoes warm.
- Enjoy.

Servings Per Recipe: 8

Timing Information:

Preparation	10 mins
Total Time	30 mins

Nutritional Information:

Calories	244.5
Fat	9.3 g
Cholesterol	0.0 mg
Sodium	14.0 mg
Carbohydrates	36.4 g
Protein	4.3 g

* Percent Daily Values are based on a 2,000 calorie diet.

Baja Bananas

Ingredients

- 8 bananas, sliced in half lengthwise
- 1 C. white sugar
- 1 tbsp cinnamon
- 1 (15 oz.) jars Mexican crema

Sauce

- 1 C. brown sugar
- 3 tbsp butter
- 3/4 C. warmed heavy cream

Directions

To prepare the caramel sauce:

- Place a heavy saucepan over low heat. Heat in it the butter.
- Add the brown sugar with whipping cream.
- Let them cook for 8 to 9 min while stirring until the sauce thickens.
- Once the time is up, turn off the heat and let the sauce cool down completely.

To prepare the bananas:

- Before you do anything, preheat the grill and grease it.
- Get a shallow plate. Stir in it the cinnamon and sugar.
- Coat the banana halves with the sugar mixture.
- Grill them for 2 to 3 min on each side until they become caramelized.
- Serve your caramelized bananas with caramel sauce and some vanilla ice cream.
- Enjoy.

Servings Per Recipe: 8

Timing Information:

Preparation	15 mins
Total Time	25 mins

Nutritional Information:

Calories	423.8
Fat	12.9 g
Cholesterol	42.0 mg
Sodium	55.7 mg
Carbohydrates	80.3 g
Protein	1.8 g

* Percent Daily Values are based on a 2,000 calorie diet.

BLACKENED WATERMELON

Ingredients

- 8 slices seedless watermelon, wedges
- 2 tbsp olive oil
- sea salt
- ground pepper

Directions

- Before you do anything, preheat the grill and grease it.
- Season the watermelon wedges with some salt. Place in a colander to drain for 35 min.
- Rinse the watermelon wedges with some water. Pat them dry with some paper towels.
- Coat the watermelon wedges with some olive oil. Grill them for 2 to 3 min on each side.
- Season your grilled watermelon with some salt and pepper then serve it warm.
- Enjoy.

Servings Per Recipe: 8

Timing Information:

Preparation	5 mins
Total Time	40 mins

Nutritional Information:

Calories	29.8
Fat	3.3 g
Cholesterol	0.0 mg
Sodium	0.0 mg
Carbohydrates	0.0 g
Protein	0.0 g

* Percent Daily Values are based on a 2,000 calorie diet.

Easy BBQ Gyros

Ingredients

- 6 -8 oz. grilled chicken breasts, diced
- 2 tbsp mayonnaise
- 2 tsp barbecue sauce
- 1 -2 tbsp blue cheese
- 2 -4 lettuce leaves
- 2 pita pockets

Directions

- Get a mixing bowl: Whisk in it the chicken, mayonnaise and BBQ sauce. Stir in the blue cheese.
- Arrange the lettuce leaves in pita pockets. Top them with chicken and cheese dressing.
- Serve your sandwiches immediately.
- Enjoy.

Servings Per Recipe: 2

Timing Information:

Preparation	5 mins
Total Time	5 mins

Nutritional Information:

Calories	374.1
Fat	8.7 g
Cholesterol	76.1 mg
Sodium	540.2 mg
Carbohydrates	39.5 g
Protein	32.3 g

* Percent Daily Values are based on a 2,000 calorie diet.

DIJON EGGPLANT AND MUSHROOMS

Ingredients

- 1/2 lb. baby zucchini, halved lengthwise
- 2 -3 baby eggplants sliced lengthwise
- 12 baby portabella mushrooms, criminis
- 1/2 lemon, juice
- 2 tsp Dijon mustard
- 2 tsp grill seasoning or dry rub
- 1 tbsp Worcestershire sauce
- 1 large garlic clove, crushed
- 3 tbsp extra virgin olive oil

Directions

- Before you do anything, preheat the grill and grease it.
- Get a mixing bowl: Whisk in it the lemon juice with mustard, grill seasoning, Worcestershire sauce, garlic and olive oil.
- Get a large zip lock bag. Place in it the veggies and pour over them the lemon dressing.
- Seal the bag and chill it in the fridge for 10 min.
- Drain the veggies and grilled until they become charred on both sides. Serve them warm.
- Enjoy.

Servings Per Recipe: 2

Timing Information:

Preparation	8 mins
Total Time	13 mins

Nutritional Information:

Calories	456.0
Fat	23.6 g
Cholesterol	0.0 mg
Sodium	206.3 mg
Carbohydrates	57.6 g
Protein	17.9 g

* Percent Daily Values are based on a 2,000 calorie diet.

COOKOUT BRUSCHETTA'S

Ingredients

- 1 French baguette
- 2 large tomatoes
- 1/2 C. gorgonzola, crumbled
- 1 C. balsamic vinegar
- 2 tbsp sugar
- 1/4 C. olive oil
- 2 tsp salt
- 1 tsp black pepper
- 2 tbsp parsley, chopped

Directions

- Before you do anything, preheat the grill and grease it.

To prepare the glaze:

- Place a heavy saucepan over medium heat. Stir in it the vinegar with sugar.
- Simmer them until they reduce by half. Turn off the heat and let it lose heat completely.

To prepare the crostini:

- Cut the baguette into 1/4 inch thick slices. Place them on a lined baking tray. Cut the tomatoes in half then place them on the baking tray as well. Coat the bread slices with tomato with olive oil. Season them with a pinch of salt and pepper.
- Place them on the grill and let them cook for 40 sec to 1 min on each side. Transfer the bread slices to a serving plate.
- Top them with grilled tomato followed by cheeses and a drizzle of glaze. Garnish them with parsley then serve them warm.
- Enjoy.

Servings Per Recipe: 10

Timing Information:

| Preparation | 30 mins |
| Total Time | 35 mins |

Nutritional Information:

Calories	129.6
Fat	7.5 g
Cholesterol	5.0 mg
Sodium	600.3 mg
Carbohydrates	12.2 g
Protein	2.6 g

* Percent Daily Values are based on a 2,000 calorie diet.

CHIPOTLE ASPARAGUS BOWLS

Ingredients

Salad

- 1 C. grilled corn, kernels removed and separated
- 1 C. grilled asparagus, sliced
- 3/4 C. red pepper, sliced
- 1 scallion, sliced

Dressing

- 1 small chipotle pepper, discard seeds
- 2 tbsp vinegar
- 1/4 C. olive oil
- 3 tbsp lime juice
- 1 clove garlic
- 1/2 tsp sugar
- 1/2 tsp thyme leave
- salt and pepper

Directions

- Get a food processor: Combine in it all the dressing ingredients. Blend them smooth.
- Get a large mixing bowl: Combine in it the corn with asparagus, pepper, and scallions.
- Add the dressing and toss them to coat.
- Place the salad in the fridge until ready to serve.
- Enjoy.

Servings Per Recipe: 4

Timing Information:

Preparation	15 mins
Total Time	15 mins

Nutritional Information:

Calories	187.6
Fat	14.2 g
Cholesterol	0.0 mg
Sodium	15.3 mg
Carbohydrates	15.3 g
Protein	2.9 g

* Percent Daily Values are based on a 2,000 calorie diet.

Appendix I: Spice Mixes, Marinades, and Dry Rubs

Carmela's Cuban Mojo (Meat Marinade)

Ingredients

- 1/4 C. olive oil
- 2 tbsp orange juice
- 2 tbsp lime juice
- 2 -4 garlic cloves, minced
- 1/2 C. chopped onion
- 2 tsp ground black pepper
- 1 tsp ground cumin
- 1 tsp salt
- 1 tsp ground ginger
- 1/2 tsp nutmeg
- 1/2 tsp cinnamon
- 1 dash ground cloves
- 1 tsp chili powder

Directions

- Get a mixing bowl: Whisk in it all the ingredients.
- Add to it your choice of meat and let it sit for at least 3 h before cooking it.
- Enjoy.

Servings per Recipe: 4

Timing Information:

Preparation	10 mins
Total Time	10 mins

Nutritional Information:

Calories	145.5
Fat	13.9g
Cholesterol	0.0mg
Sodium	595.3mg
Carbohydrates	5.8g
Protein	0.7g

* Percent Daily Values are based on a 2,000 calorie diet.

SIMPLE HOMEMADE RED CURRY (CHILI) PASTE (THAILAND STYLE)

To prepare a red curry paste use red chilies for a green curry paste use green chilies.

Ingredients
- ¼ C. chopped scallion
- ¼ C. chopped fresh cilantro
- 2 tbsps minced garlic
- 2 tbsps grated fresh gingerroot
- 1 tbsp freshly grated lemon rinds
- 1 tbsp brown sugar
- 1-2 fresh red chilies or 1 -2 green chili, minced
- 3 tbsps fresh lemon juice
- 1 tbsp ground coriander
- 1 tsp turmeric
- ½ tsp salt

Directions
- Add the following your food processor: scallion, cilantro, garlic, ginger root, lemons / lime, brown sugar, chilies, lemon / lime juice, coriander, turmeric, and salt.
- Process and pulse everything until it becomes a smooth paste.
- Enjoy.

Servings per Recipe: 1

Timing Information:

Preparation	10 mins
Total Time	10 mins

Nutritional Information:

Calories	300.4
Fat	3.5 g
Cholesterol	0 mg
Sodium	2368.8 mg
Carbohydrates	71.1 g
Protein	7.5 g

* Percent Daily Values are based on a 2,000 calorie diet.

CREOLE SEASONING

Ingredients

- 2 tbsps onion powder
- 2 tbsps garlic powder
- 2 tbsps dried oregano
- 2 tbsps dried basil
- 1 tbsp dried thyme
- 1 tbsp black pepper
- 1 tbsp white pepper
- 1 tbsp cayenne pepper
- 5 tbsps paprika
- 3 tbsps salt

Directions

- Get a bowl, combine: salt, onion powder, paprika, garlic powder, cayenne, oregano, white pepper, thyme, black pepper, and basil.
- Stir the spices evenly then place them in a shaker or spice container.
- Enjoy.

Servings per Recipe: 20

Timing Information:

Preparation	
Cooking	5 m
Total Time	5 m

Nutritional Information:

Calories	16 kcal
Fat	< 0.4 g
Carbohydrates	< 3.4g
Protein	0.7 g
Cholesterol	0 mg
Sodium	1048 mg

* Percent Daily Values are based on a 2,000 calorie diet.

TUCSON RUB FOR MEATS

Ingredients

- 4 tsp kosher salt
- 2 tsp ground cumin
- 2 tsp chili powder
- 2 tsp dried cilantro
- 2 tsp dried onion flakes

Directions

- Get a small mixing bowl. Mix in it all the spices.
- Massage the mixture into the chicken pieces. Let them sit in the fridge for 60 min.
- Grill them to your liking.
- Enjoy.

Servings Per Recipe: 1

Timing Information:

Preparation	5 mins
Total Time	1 hr 5 mins

Nutritional Information:

Calories	169.4
Fat	7.1 g
Cholesterol	0.0 mg
Sodium	28300.2 mg
Carbohydrates	28.3 g
Protein	7.7 g

* Percent Daily Values are based on a 2,000 calorie diet.

THANKS FOR READING! JOIN THE CLUB AND KEEP ON COOKING WITH 6 MORE COOKBOOKS....

http://bit.ly/1TdrStv

To grab the box sets simply follow the link mentioned above, or tap one of book covers.

This will take you to a page where you can simply enter your email address and a PDF version of the box sets will be emailed to you.

Hope you are ready for some serious cooking!

http://bit.ly/1TdrStv

COME ON...
LET'S BE FRIENDS :)

We adore our readers and love connecting with them socially.

Like BookSumo on Facebook and let's get social!

Facebook

And also check out the BookSumo Cooking Blog.

Food Lover Blog

CPSIA information can be obtained
at www.ICGtesting.com
Printed in the USA
FSHW010136211218
54581FS

9 781724 578457